The
TITANIC
SINKS!

The
TITANIC
SINKS!

by Thomas Conklin

A STEPPING STONE BOOK™
Random House 🏠 New York

For the unsinkable Laura Christine

Copyright © 1997 by Thomas Conklin. All rights reserved under International and Pan-American Copyright Conventions. Published in the United States by Random House Children's Books, a division of Random House, Inc., New York, and simultaneously in Canada by Random House of Canada Limited, Toronto.

www.randomhouse.com/kids

Library of Congress Cataloging-in-Publication Data
Conklin, Thomas, 1960–
The Titanic sinks! / by Thomas Conklin.
   p. cm.
SUMMARY: Recounts the story of how the world's biggest, safest ship sank on its first trip.
ISBN 0-679-88606-0 (pbk.) — ISBN 0-679-98606-5 (lib. bdg.)
1. Titanic (Steamship)—Juvenile literature. 2. Shipwrecks—North Atlantic Ocean—Juvenile literature. [1. Titanic (Steamship). 2. Shipwrecks.]
I. Title. G530.T6C67 1997 910'.91634—dc21 97-4060

Printed in the United States of America 19 18 17 16

RANDOM HOUSE and colophon are registered trademarks and A STEPPING STONE BOOK and colophon are trademarks of Random House, Inc.

AUTHOR'S NOTE

This book is based on facts. All the events described here are true accounts of real people.

In some cases, I have written dialogue or imagined what the passengers aboard the *Titanic* might have thought or felt.

—Thomas Conklin

9NTRODUCTION

In late April 1912, Mayor William J. Gaynor of New York City received a postcard from Europe. It was dated April 11.

The front of the postcard was a picture of a huge ocean liner plowing through the waves. The ship had four large smokestacks and a vast black hull. It was the Royal Mail Steamer *Titanic*.

Mayor Gaynor turned over the postcard and read the message scrawled on the back:

"Guess you had better chain up the Statue of Liberty to a skyscraper on Fifth Avenue…Better instruct the United States fleet to tow her in, or I guess New York will be wiped off the map."

The postcard was signed by Seaton Blake, a steward on the *Titanic*. Blake had mailed his message to the mayor just as the ship started its first voyage from Europe to New York.

Blake thought that the *Titanic* was so big and powerful that it would "swallow up" the Statue of Liberty as it passed by. After all, the *Titanic* was the greatest ocean liner ever.

To build the *Titanic* took almost three years. Its owner, the White Star Line, had spared no expense in making this the best ship afloat. When all the work was done, the *Titanic* had cost more than $10 million—a mind-boggling amount back in 1912.

From front to back the *Titanic* measured 882 feet— almost as long as three football fields. The steel plates of the *Titanic* were held in place by more than 3 million metal rivets. The rivets alone weighed 1,200 tons. The ship's mammoth rudder was as tall as a house, and weighed a hundred tons. The *Titanic* had three giant propellers, powered by steam engines as strong as 46,000 horses!

The ship was designed with two goals in mind—comfort and stability. Advertisements for the *Titanic* described it as "the most sumptuous palace afloat." Newspapers called it "the wonder ship," "the last word in luxury," and "the millionaires' special."

As long as four city blocks and as tall as an eleven-story building, the *Titanic* was incredible. For its first voyage, the ship was scheduled to travel from Southampton, England, to New York.

But the *Titanic* never made it to New York.

By the time Blake's postcard was delivered to Mayor Gaynor, the *Titanic* was in pieces on the ocean floor, under two and a half miles of freezing salt water. More than 1,500 people—including Seaton Blake—had died along with the ship.

The entire world was shocked when the *Titanic* went down, only five days into its first voyage. Instead of signifying comfort and stability, the *Titanic* came to stand for disaster and terror.

Today, eighty-five years after the wreck of the *Titanic*, people are still fascinated by the death of the great ship. What was it like to sail on the *Titanic*? What happened that fateful night when it sank beneath the waves? How did anyone survive the terrible accident?

And, most important of all, how could such a disaster have happened?

ONE

The steam whistles of the R.M.S. *Titanic* bellowed a farewell as the immense ship eased into the harbor channel of Southampton in England.

It was an awesome sight. The crowd on the dock ran alongside the mighty *Titanic* as it slowly made its way to sea. On the docks, people yelled and waved handkerchiefs at the hundreds of lucky passengers on board. Passengers called good-byes and last messages from the *Titanic*'s many decks. Far up on the boat deck, the ship's band played cheerful music, which added to the excitement.

The *Titanic* passed two ocean liners, the *Oceanic* and *New York,* as it moved down the channel. They seemed like toy boats next to the massive *Titanic*. The *Titanic*'s four huge funnels, or smokestacks, loomed over those of the other ships. The crowd on the dock cheered with pride as the colossal, queenly *Titanic* headed to the open sea on its first voyage.

Then, suddenly, a sound like gunfire echoed from the decks of the *New York*. Six hawsers, the steel cables that anchored the ocean liner in place, broke off and snaked through the air toward the dock. The panicked crowd screamed and ducked.

Onboard the *Titanic,* passengers crowded the ship's rail and watched in horror as the *New York* drifted across the water. The smaller ship headed straight for the *Titanic*'s black hull, as if drawn by an invisible force. Officers on the *New York* shouted orders, and its sailors rushed to and fro. They draped mats over the side of the boat, hoping to soften the inevitable collision.

It seemed as though nothing could prevent a crash, but then the *Titanic* took charge. Its pilot ordered the port engine to surge. The engine rumbled with power, forcing water away from the *Titanic*. The swelling water pushed the smaller ship away at the last possible moment.

Passengers on the *Titanic* sighed with relief as a pair of tugboats came alongside the *New York* and towed it out of their ship's path. After a short delay, the *Titanic* was again on its way.

Many of the *Titanic*'s passengers were impressed by the officers in charge of their ship. Their quick thinking had avoided the accident. The passengers were also proud to be the first on board this "unsinkable" ship. The *Titanic* was the largest moving object on the surface of the planet. It was so big it could pull and push another ocean liner as if it were a rubber duck.

As the passengers settled into their cabins for the voyage across the ocean, one woman turned to the crewman carrying her luggage.

"Is this ship really unsinkable?" she asked.

"Yes, lady," the crewman replied with confidence. "God himself could not sink this ship."

TWO

Thursday, April 11, 1912
Dusk

After that rocky start, the first leg of the *Titanic's* voyage turned out to be smooth sailing. The ocean liner arrived at Cherbourg, France, on Wednesday, April 10—right on schedule. There, dozens of passengers joined the ship, including John Jacob Astor and his young wife, Madeleine. Astor was one of the richest men alive. He and his bride had spent months honeymooning in Europe. Now they were returning to their home in New York.

On Thursday, the *Titanic* steamed to Queenstown, Ireland. There, the ship dropped its anchors—all thirty-one tons of them—and its final passengers came aboard. Most of those who joined the ship at Queenstown were emigrants, leaving Ireland to start new lives in the United States.

Soon the *Titanic* was off again, steaming quickly away from the lovely rounded mountains of Ireland's western coast. Nothing but the dark green ocean lay ahead of the ship as it made its way into the beautiful scarlet sunset.

One man on board, J. Bruce Ismay, was filled with doubt as the *Titanic* entered the open sea. Ismay was managing director of the White Star Line, the company that owned the R.M.S. *Titanic*. He was personally overseeing the *Titanic*'s first voyage, as he did with all of his company's ships.

Ismay was *not* worried about the ship's safety.

Are the mattresses firm enough? Ismay wondered. *Will the new electric potato peeler help the galley crew keep up the pace? Were cigar holders added to the first-class bathrooms, as I ordered?*

Ismay's mind was on the thousand and one details that would make the *Titanic* perfect in its passengers' eyes. He considered it his job to make sure that every detail was taken care of.

Despite his concerns for the comfort of his passengers, Ismay could not help but be filled with pride. The *Titanic* was his company's greatest achievement.

Ismay's father had founded the White Star Line more

than forty years before. The company's steamships took people across the Atlantic between Europe and North America. It was a big business, and the White Star Line had a lot of competition. In recent years, other companies had built ships that could make the trip faster than White Star's.

By 1907, Ismay had settled on a strategy for beating the competition. Other companies might run faster ships—but White Star would offer nervous travelers the biggest, most comfortable, *safest* ships in the world.

On May 11, 1911, the White Star Line launched the first of its huge new ships: the *Olympic*. Passengers were awed by its size and comfort. Ismay vowed that the line's next ship, the *Titanic*, would be even better.

Now, as he stood on the deck of the *Titanic*, Ismay knew he owned the world's finest ship, with the most skilled crew available aboard.

Commanding the ship was Edward J. Smith, one of the best-loved and most respected ship captains in the world. He was crowning his twenty-five-year career by guiding the magnificent *Titanic* on her maiden voyage. After this last trip, he planned to retire. Captain Smith was tall, broad, and handsome, with a snow-white beard. Everyone called him E.J.

"I have never been in any accident of any sort worth speaking about," Captain Smith said in an interview shortly before setting sail on the *Titanic*. "I never saw a wreck and never have been wrecked," he added, modestly describing his record.

Captain Smith had every reason to believe that this voyage would be a smooth one. He had 397 officers, engineers, and crewmen under his command. Each one was an experienced seaman. Also, the *Titanic* boasted all the latest safety features. In fact, the technical journal *Shipbuilder* had declared the *Titanic* to be "virtually unsinkable."

The *Titanic* had ten decks, stacked like the stories of a building. On the very top of the ship was the boat deck, where first- and second-class passengers could stroll and enjoy the sea air. The ship's bridge, which provided its officers with a sweeping view of the sea, stood at the front of the *Titanic*'s boat deck.

The boat deck was also where the lifeboats were stored. The *Titanic* carried sixteen lifeboats and four "collapsible" mini-lifeboats—four more lifeboats than British law required of a ship her size.

The other decks were designated A through G, with A being the uppermost. On these decks were the cabins, common rooms, lounges, smoking rooms, storage areas, galleys, and every other space used by the 2,200 passengers and crew members.

Below its upper decks, the *Titanic* was divided into a

series of watertight compartments by fifteen steel walls, called bulkheads, that ran from one side of the ship to the other. The bulkheads extended as high as E-deck, well above the waterline. To get through the bulkheads, passengers and crew members passed through watertight doors that could be sealed instantly with a single switch on the ship's bridge. In the unlikely event that the *Titanic* sprang a leak, up to four compartments could take on water without causing the ship to sink.

The bottom deck was called the tank top. Here, dozens of "greasers" made sure the ship's three huge engines were greased and ran smoothly.

The tank top was also where stokers shoveled coal into the 149 furnaces fueling the *Titanic*'s twenty-nine enormous boilers. The boilers heated water and turned it to steam. The pressure of the steam powered the engines, which turned the *Titanic*'s three huge propellers.

Finally, the very bottom of the *Titanic* was a double-hulled keel. Even if the hull were punctured, water would be kept out of the rest of the ship.

All in all, the *Titanic* was as shipshape as any vessel afloat in 1912.

Still, Captain Smith knew that not everything was perfect with his ship or its crew. It had taken quick thinking to avoid the collision with the *New York* in Southampton. And much of his crew had joined the *Titanic* just before it

THREE

Friday, April 12, 1912
Morning

The skies were clear and sunny as the *Titanic* made its way across the Atlantic Ocean on Friday and Saturday. In that perfect weather, passengers enjoyed life aboard the world's greatest ship. For first- and second-class passengers, the *Titanic* was more like a luxury hotel than an oceangoing vessel. Even most of the passengers in third class found the *Titanic* more comfortable than their homes on shore had been.

Seventeen-year-old Jack Thayer was traveling with his parents in first class. Jack's father was a wealthy railroad executive, and his family was prominent in Philadelphia society. The Thayers were able to take advantage of the best the *Titanic* had to offer. One of the 518 stewards on board was assigned specifically to Jack and his family. It was the steward's job to take care of their every need. He polished their shoes, picked up their laundry, and called them to meals.

Most of the 337 first-class passengers of the *Titanic* were used to that sort of service. Many of the wealthiest people in the world were on board. Their quarters and meeting rooms were in the central part of the ship, where the ship's engines were the quietest.

The Thayers stayed in elegant staterooms, like a suite in a luxury hotel. Jack had a room to himself, and his parents' room was connected to a comfortable sitting room. The only telltale signs that the Thayers were at sea were the bright yellow life jackets stowed in each cabin.

For Jack, traveling on the *Titanic* was an exciting new adventure. He couldn't wait to leave the stateroom and explore the ship's other rooms and passages.

On the first-class section of the boat deck, Jack saw the ship's gymnasium and met instructor T. W. McCawley. The spry little Englishman loved to show off the exercise bicycles, mechanical horses and camels, and other equipment to help first-class passengers keep fit. On the deck outside the gymnasium were a few of the ship's lifeboats. They were stowed beneath the small cranes, called davits, that could lower them to the ocean.

Next, Jack wandered down the Grand Staircase, the ship's most impressive feature. The ceiling above the staircase was covered with a domed glass skylight, which allowed the sun's rays to shine upon the polished wood paneling and the gilded, hand-carved stair rails. The staircase led down from the boat deck all the way to D-deck, four flights below. If a passenger wasn't in the mood to walk, he or she could take one of the three elevators opposite the stairs.

Each deck in first class offered attractions to please the richest, most demanding passenger. First-class passengers could relax in the large lounge on A-deck. The lounge was filled with fine furniture; its hand-carved paneling was lit by brass sconces and chandeliers.

There was also a plush smoking lounge, where passengers like Major Archie Butt, President William Howard Taft's closest aide, sat up late into the night playing cards and smoking cigars. One deck beneath the smoking lounge was the Café Parisien, which was designed to look like a Paris bistro. The elegant first-class dining saloon, where passengers enjoyed eight-course gourmet meals, was the largest room afloat.

What if a passenger overdid it at the dining table? There were plenty of chances to work it off. Besides the gymnasium up on the boat deck, the Titanic also had a steambath, a full-size squash court, even a heated swimming pool. Never before had there been such a ship. The *Titanic* was the most amazing thing Jack Thayer had ever seen.

Twelve-year-old Ruth Becker was not as impressed with the *Titanic* as Jack and her second-class shipmates were. Maybe that was because Ruth's parents were missionaries, and the family had already made many sea voyages. Also, as second-class passengers, the Beckers were not allowed to enter the ship's best sections.

Still, second class on the *Titanic* was as comfortable as first class on most other ships. Ruth shared a large cabin on F-deck with her mother, Nellie, her four-year-old sister, Marion, and her baby brother, Richard. Allen Becker, Ruth's father, was in India and could not make the family trip.

Up two flights of stairs, on D-deck, was the second-class dining saloon. There, Ruth and the 270 other second-class passengers ate delicious meals on long tables covered with starched linen tablecloths. When she got bored, Ruth could go up to the second-class library on C-deck. This handsome, paneled room had hundreds of books for passengers to choose from. They could also check their ship's progress, which was shown on a map of the Atlantic Ocean posted in the library. Outside the library was a closed-in walkway, or promenade, which became the unofficial playground for children in second class.

Most passengers, adults and children alike, socialized and made friends with their fellow passengers. But Ruth, a mature, quiet girl, kept to herself. She took it upon herself to look after baby Richard, who was sick.

Unlike Ruth, third-class passenger Daniel Buckley liked to make friends and have fun. But it wasn't as easy for the twenty-one-year-old to mingle with the other passengers. Buckley was leaving Ireland to move to the United States. His cramped quarters, which he shared with three other young men, were on G-deck, the lowest deck for passengers, in the very front of the *Titanic*. Unlike the rooms for first- and second-class passengers, third-class quarters were plain and simple, with stark white walls and wooden bunks.

To get fresh air or exercise, Daniel had to climb three flights of stairs to D-deck. There, he could stroll out on the forward well deck of the ship. Looming three stories above and behind the well deck were the windows of the ship's bridge. In front was the tall mast holding the ship's crow's nest. Beyond that was the ship's bow, plowing through the cold Atlantic.

Unfortunately, there was not much to do in the well deck, and the April wind whipping off the Atlantic could be bitterly cold. To visit the warm and inviting third-class lounge, smoking room, and promenade, Daniel and the others had to walk all the way to the stern of the *Titanic*.

In these common rooms, the 712 third-class passengers could gather to sit on plain wooden benches, talk and play cards, or sing and dance. Unlike first and second class, where the passengers were mostly English and American, third class buzzed with many languages. People from England, Ireland, France, Poland, Italy, Scandinavia, the Middle East, and Asia all shared the third-class lounge. Many large families, along with single men and women, were glad to join the maiden voyage of the *Titanic*. For most, it was their first trip across the ocean, and they expected it to be their last. They were on their way to start new lives in America.

At least Daniel and the third-class passengers could stretch their legs as they walked through the ship. That wasn't the case for twenty-two-year-old Harold Bride.

Harold Bride was the junior wireless-telegraph operator aboard the *Titanic*. His life revolved around the tiny wireless office tucked behind the ship's bridge.

There, he took turns with the senior wireless operator, Jack Phillips. The *Titanic* had the most powerful radio of any ship afloat, and could reach ships hundreds of miles away. The wireless operator on duty sat wearing headphones, either writing down radio messages received in Morse code, or tapping out messages to be sent. It was Bride and Phillips's job to keep the wireless going twenty-four hours a day.

When he wasn't busy at work, Bride would crawl

through the curtain separating the wireless office from a tiny bunk alongside it. There, he would sleep soundly until his next shift.

For Bride, working on a huge luxury ship like the *Titanic* was no different from his previous jobs on other ships. In fact, most of the messages Bride sent were trivial greetings from passengers to friends ashore.

If Bride had any complaint, it was that he didn't have much to do.

That would soon change.

₵OUR

Saturday, April 13, 1912
Afternoon

"Everything is going well," Bruce Ismay told Captain Smith.

Passengers relaxing in the first-class reception room couldn't help but overhear the two men talking. It was early Saturday afternoon, and the *Titanic* was in the middle of the Atlantic Ocean. So far, their voyage had been perfect. The weather, although cold, had been clear. The sea was calm, and the *Titanic* was making excellent time.

The passengers were glad to hear their captain and the owner of the ship sounding so confident.

Bruce Ismay and Captain Smith compared the *Titanic*'s performance with that of its sister ship, the *Olympic*. In its first day at sea, the *Titanic* had covered 484 miles. The *Olympic* had traveled 458 miles on its first day. The second day, the *Titanic* had fallen behind a bit. It had made 519 miles, compared with the *Olympic's* 524.

So far, the *Titanic* was steaming as fast as the *Olympic* had on its first voyage. Could the *Titanic* pick up the pace and outdo her sister ship?

"We made a better run today than we did yesterday," Ismay told Captain Smith. "We will make a better run tomorrow. Things are working smoothly, the machinery is bearing the test, the boilers are working well."

Ismay, growing excited, brought his fist down onto the arm of his chair. "We will beat the *Olympic* and get in to New York on Tuesday!" he declared.

Although the *Titanic's* boilers and engines were performing well, not all of the ship's systems were perfect. Late in the day on Saturday, Harold Bride and Jack Phillips noticed something wrong with the ship's wireless. Before long, it had broken down completely. The two men worked feverishly to find the trouble. All Saturday night and into the early morning hours on Sunday they fiddled with the set. Meanwhile, passengers' messages piled up in their "in" basket.

Finally, at about five o'clock on Sunday morning, Phillips and Bride got the wireless set running again and began to send out the huge backlog of messages. If anything gave them a sense of relief, it was knowing that soon they would come within range of North America. This meant they could send their messages directly to a wireless station. The messages would be passed immediately to their destination, instead of being relayed from ship to ship.

As the *Titanic's* passengers woke up on Sunday morning, they were greeted by beautiful weather. Only one thing spoiled the fine day: The air had grown colder, so most passengers had to pass the time indoors.

Daniel Buckley and some third-class passengers braved the chill to come out on the rear well deck, behind the boat deck. There, in the bright, cold sunshine, they played a skipping game similar to hopscotch. Another passenger came out with a set of bagpipes on which he played sad tunes.

Meanwhile, first-class passenger Archibald Gracie was feeling restless after two days with no exercise. Early Sunday morning, he headed down to G-deck, where he played a vigorous game of squash, then went for a swim in the heated pool just around the corner from the court. The warm water was soothing and comfortable—unlike the icy ocean, kept out by the steel hull of the ship, less than an inch thick, which Gracie could almost touch from the side of the pool.

In the second-class dining saloon, Ruth Becker was growing to like the *Titanic*. The best part about it was that everything was new. Ruth liked knowing that when she sat down to her first meal aboard the ship, she was the very first person ever to eat off the plate in front of her. The sheets on the bed in her cabin were crisp and fresh. She was the first person ever to use them! Even the carpets in the lounges and dining saloon smelled new.

After breakfast, Ruth and the rest of the Becker family stayed in the dining saloon for Sunday services. The highlight of the service was the hymns. This Sunday, the room was filled with the sounds of the passengers singing "O God, Our Help in Ages Past."

Up in the officers' quarters, Captain Smith was faced with a decision. There had been a lifeboat drill scheduled for 11:30 on Sunday morning. For the drill, each crew member would have to proceed to the boat deck and take his position by the emergency lifeboats. As captain, E.J. knew how important it was for his crew to be prepared for an emergency. Still, the *Titanic* was obviously a very safe ship. The likelihood that anyone would ever need the lifeboats was slim. What was more, the weather had turned colder. To hold a lifeboat drill out on the open boat deck would expose his crew to the freezing wind.

Finally, if he held the drill as scheduled, Captain Smith would not be able to conduct Sunday services in the first-

₵IVE

Sunday, April 14, 1912
Early Afternoon

To: Capt. Smith, Titanic

*Have had mod. var. winds and clear fine weather since
leaving. Greek steamer* Athinai *reports passing icebergs
and large quantity of field ice today....*

This warning about ice, the second one of the day, was
received on the *Titanic* at 1:40 on Sunday afternoon. After
he read the telegram, Captain Smith headed for A-deck.
The earlier warning was already posted in the chart
room, where all of the ship's officers could see it.

As he walked down the promenade, Captain Smith
bumped into Bruce Ismay. Without a word, Smith handed

the telegram to the director of the White Star Line. Ismay glanced at the telegram and stuck it in his pocket.

The spring of 1912 was a dangerous season on the Atlantic Ocean. The winter had been unusually warm, so more icebergs than normal had broken free of the great glaciers around Greenland. These icebergs were drifting south into the shipping routes.

Already, a few days into its voyage, the *Titanic* had received many warnings about icebergs. To be on the safe side, Captain Smith had ordered that the ship take a route ten miles south of the normal shipping route. Captain Smith was confident that this more southern route would avoid danger.

Most passengers spent the chilly Sunday afternoon indoors, playing cards or visiting with friends, old and new. In first class, Jack Thayer's mother spent the afternoon trying to cheer up her friend Emily Ryerson. Mrs. Ryerson was terribly depressed. She and her husband were hurrying home from a European vacation to attend the funeral of their son, who had been killed in a car crash only a week before.

The two women sat quietly on deck chairs in the enclosed promenade on A-deck. Just as the sun was beginning to set, Bruce Ismay joined them and asked Mrs. Ryerson how she was doing. Then Ismay began hunting in his pockets.

"We are in among the icebergs," he declared, taking Captain Smith's telegram and showing it to the women. Ismay explained that they were planning to light two more boilers later that night, in order to pick up the pace. That way, they would pass through the dangerous waters quickly. They would also arrive in New York early "and surprise everyone."

After chatting with Mrs. Ryerson and Mrs. Thayer, Ismay returned the telegram to Captain Smith so he could post it in the officers' chart room.

At that time, Second Officer Charles H. Lightoller was in command of the ship. His watch would last from six P.M. until ten P.M. Working from the previous warnings, Lightoller had already calculated that the *Titanic* would reach the area where ice had been spotted at about eleven that night.

As he gazed from the bridge onto the open sea, Lightoller saw an ocean as still and flat as a sheet of glass. The sunset he peered into was a spectacular blaze of orange between the clear, calm sea and the cloudless purple sky. Everything was well under control.

Lightoller temporarily turned over command of the bridge to First Officer William Murdoch in order to grab a quick supper. Out on the boat deck, Lightoller shuddered and wrapped his coat tightly around his body. As the sun dropped, so did the temperature.

Around the corner in the wireless office, Harold Bride was letting his radio's alternator cool off as he did some paperwork. At 7:30, when he turned the wireless set back on, Bride overheard a message being sent to another ship:

6:30 P.M., apparent time, ship; latitude 42.3 north, longitude 49.9 west. Three large bergs five miles to southward of us.

Bride took the message to the bridge immediately. The *Titanic* forged ahead, its speed unchanged.

At about the same time, Jack Thayer was getting dressed for dinner. It was a special night for the Thayer family: They were dining with Captain Smith and Major Butt, the aide to President Taft.

That night, the first-class restaurant looked like one of the finest restaurants in the richest sections of London, New York, or Paris. The wealthy diners were dressed in their very best. The men wore crisp, dark evening suits, with starched white shirts, black bow ties, and tuxedo jackets or formal jackets with tails. The women wore sparkling jewelry and long gowns made of the best silks and satins.

The menu that night offered an eight-course feast. Diners could order oysters, filet mignon, lamb, roast duckling, roast squab, pâté de foie gras, and more. A different bottle of fine wine was poured with each course.

Of course, Captain Smith politely declined to drink any alcohol.

In the second-class dining saloon, Ruth Becker and her family had a much simpler menu of fish, chicken, lamb, or turkey.

After the meal was over and the dishes cleared away, the second-class passengers settled down for an evening of wholesome entertainment, singing hymns. The Reverend Ernest Carter, a British passenger, had organized the sing-along. He took requests from passengers and announced the hymns to be sung. Before each one began, Reverend Carter told everyone about the hymn's author and why it was written.

The high point of the evening was the singing of "Lead Kindly Light," a solo performed by passenger Marion Wright. Before she sang, Reverend Carter explained that the hymn was inspired by a shipwreck in the Atlantic Ocean. Another hymn selected was "For Those in Peril on the Sea." The room was unusually hushed during this last hymn. Many men and women were overcome with emotion, and wept openly during the song.

Back in the third-class section, the passengers weren't eating lavish meals or singing hymns. Some had formed an impromptu band and played music in the lounge. Others started dancing.

Just as the party was warming up, the music suddenly

stopped. A young woman in the corner screamed with terror, "No! No! No!"

A crowd gathered around the woman and asked her what was wrong. Terrified, she pointed to a dark corner.

"It's...it's...a *rat*!" she exclaimed.

Laughing as other women shrieked and jumped onto chairs, the men chased the rat from the corner and across the floor. The music started up again.

Few passengers ventured outside into the freezing night.

In the wireless office, Jack Phillips had taken over for Harold Bride. Phillips sat hunched over the desk, working hard. The *Titanic* had at last sailed into range of Cape Race, a station on Newfoundland. Phillips was busy sending the passengers' dozens and dozens of messages to the mainland.

At around 9:30, Phillips received the following message from another ship:

Ice report. In latitude 42 north to 41.25 north, longitude 49 west to longitude 50.3 west. Saw much heavy pack ice and great number of icebergs, also field ice. Weather good, clear.

Phillips was tired after staying up all night to fix the wireless. He still had a huge stack of messages to get through. This was just one of many messages about ice that he and Harold Bride had already sent up to the bridge. He decided it could wait.

Phillips wired the ship to thank them for the warning, then put it under a paperweight on his desk. He would take it to the bridge—later, when he had the time.

Phillips had no way of knowing that the warning described an ice field dead ahead—and that the *Titanic* was steaming into it at high speed.

SIX

Sunday, April 14, 1912
10:00 P.M.

The thermometer outside the *Titanic*'s bridge read thirty-one degrees Fahrenheit. It was ten P.M. when First Officer Murdoch took over command of the ship from Second Officer Lightoller. Captain Smith had just checked in to make sure everything was all right before retiring to his cabin for the night.

"We will be up around the ice somewhere about eleven o'clock," Lightoller said, reminding Murdoch of the ice warnings. With that, he left the bridge.

First Officer Murdoch took his position on the darkened boat deck and peered at the ocean ahead. The water was as smooth as a pond. There was no moon that night, but the stars twinkled brightly through the clear, cold sky.

First Officer Murdoch wasn't the only one staring out to sea. High above the ship, lookouts Frederick Fleet and Reginald Lee scanned the water from the crow's nest. The crow's nest was the coldest spot on the ship. It was exposed to the open air, on a mast directly in front of the ship's bridge.

Fleet and Lee tried not to be distracted by the cold. It was their job to keep watch for icebergs, ships, and other objects that might stray into the *Titanic*'s path. Both men knew that the ship had been warned about icebergs. They also knew that ice would be extremely hard to see under the conditions that night. Without a moon, the sea was darker than usual. And in the perfectly calm water, they couldn't see the white foam of waves breaking against the icebergs.

One thing would have helped Fleet and Lee: binoculars. The lookouts in the crow's nest were not supplied with them. The men had to rely on their own eyesight to spot trouble ahead. It was the *Titanic*'s first voyage, and the crew had been in a hurry to get ready. Naturally a few details had been overlooked.

Throughout the ship, passengers were settling into their cabins for a good night's sleep. Only the first- and second-class lounges and smoking rooms were full. There, men continued playing cards, although many of their fellow passengers thought it was wrong to do so on Sunday.

In the wireless office, Phillips continued sending messages to Cape Race. Suddenly, a message burst in his headphones at full volume:

Say, old man, we are stopped and surrounded by ice.

The message had come from another ship, the *Californian*. It came in so loud and clear that the *Californian* had to be very close by. Phillips, who was already tired and had been startled by the sudden message, hastily tapped out a reply:

Shut up! Shut up! I am busy.

A few miles away, the telegraph operator for the *Californian* listened to Phillips's rude response. He stayed on the line for a few minutes and heard the messages being sent from the *Titanic*. Then he turned off his wireless set and went to bed.

By this time, it was past 11:30. The *Titanic* was quiet. Almost every passenger had gone to bed. Even the card games in the smoking lounges were winding down. As the passengers settled in for the night, many noticed that the vibrations from the ship's engines were stronger than ever. The *Titanic* was picking up speed.

In the crow's nest, both Fleet and Lee were eager for their watch to end at midnight. They counted the minutes as they stared intently into the frigid blackness ahead.

Fleet squinted. He noticed a fine haze on the water, looming directly ahead of the *Titanic*. He peered intently into the mist.

Then, suddenly, he saw it, in the middle of the mist: a large black object, dead ahead. It could be only one thing.

Fleet reached out and rang the warning bell three times. "There's ice ahead," he told Lee, as he grabbed the telephone linked directly to the bridge.

"Is there anyone there?" Fleet barked into the telephone.

"Yes," replied Sixth Officer James Moody, who was stationed by the phone in the bridge. "What do you see?"

"Iceberg right ahead!" Fleet said.

"Thank you!" Sixth Officer Moody replied, and hung up the phone.

"Iceberg right ahead!" Moody called out to the dark bridge.

First Officer Murdoch, in command of the ship, immediately gave orders.

"Hard a' starboard!" he called to the helmsman, who manned the ship's wheel. At the same time, Murdoch signaled the engine room to "full speed astern," which would put the *Titanic*'s engines in reverse.

"Hard a' starboard. The helm is hard over, sir," Moody called when the order had been followed.

First Officer Murdoch had hoped that by reversing the engines and turning the ship to its port—left—side, he would steer the *Titanic* clear of the iceberg.

Once his orders were given, all Murdoch could do was wait and watch. Seconds ticked by as the iceberg loomed closer…and closer.

In the crow's nest, Fleet and Lee watched in horror as the ship neared the iceberg. The *Titanic* was still headed straight for the huge blue mass.

At the last possible moment, the *Titanic*'s bow began to swing to port. The pale iceberg slipped along the ship's starboard side.

The *Titanic* was going to miss the iceberg!

SEVEN

Sunday, April 14, 1912
11:40 P.M.

First Officer Murdoch's heart soared. His orders had worked! The *Titanic* was not going to ram the iceberg!

But then Murdoch heard a low, ominous crunch. The side of the *Titanic* was scraping against the iceberg.

Most of the passengers didn't realize that the ship was hitting the iceberg. One person who did hear the collision said it sounded like a giant skate slicing along the ice. Another thought it sounded as if the ship had rolled over a thousand marbles. To another, it felt as if someone had drawn a giant finger along the side of the ship.

To the crew members on the bridge, the sound meant one thing: trouble.

First Officer Murdoch immediately rang an alarm and threw the switch sealing every watertight door on the ship.

"Note the time!" Murdoch called out, his voice steady and calm. "Record it in the log!"

It was exactly 11:40 P.M.

As the iceberg scraped along the side of the *Titanic,* huge sheets of ice fell onto the ship's forward well deck. Few people were up to see the collision. In the first- and second-class smoking lounges, a handful of diehard card players were still at it when they felt the mild bump of the iceberg. They rushed outside just in time to see the iceberg pass by the side of the ship, its jagged, pointed top looming over the *Titanic*'s boat deck.

When the ship had passed the iceberg and they thought the excitement was over, the men returned to their card games.

Captain Smith rushed to the bridge moments after the accident.

"What have we struck?" he asked.

"An iceberg, sir," Murdoch replied. "I put her hard a' starboard and run the engines full astern, but it was too close. She hit it."

"Close the watertight doors," Smith ordered.

"The watertight doors are closed, sir."

Captain Smith gazed out at the calm sea. His ship had

been damaged— but how badly? He ordered the engines to half-speed, then, a few moments later, had them stopped. He demanded damage reports from every officer and from the ship's carpenter.

Within minutes, Captain Smith began hearing the bad news. The forepeak tank, the compartment at the very bow of the ship, was taking on water. The crew also reported that the ship had a gash in its side as far back as Boiler Room Number 5. The boiler rooms were already filled with eight feet of churning green seawater. And the water was rising—fast. The ship's engineers were doing their best to pump the water out of the boiler rooms. But it was a losing battle.

On G-deck, one level above the boiler rooms, mailroom clerks were desperately dragging mailbags into the post office from the storeroom below. The storeroom was flooding rapidly.

The damage reports outdid Captain Smith's worst fears. First, he apprised White Star director Bruce Ismay of the situation. Then he met with the one man who knew the *Titanic* better than anyone else. That man was Thomas Andrews, the chief designer for Harland and Wolff, the company that had built the *Titanic*. Andrews knew the ship inside and out. Together, he and Captain Smith went over the blueprints.

From the reports, it was clear that the *Titanic* had

been damaged in its first six watertight compartments. More than 300 feet of the ship had been opened to the sea. Andrews pointed out that the "watertight" compartments were not, in fact, sealed at the top. Once a compartment was filled, water could spill over the top of its bulkheads and begin filling the next compartment.

The ship had been designed to float with any three of its compartments flooded. It might even stay afloat with four compartments flooded. But with its first six compartments flooding, the *Titanic* was doomed. The weight of the water filling the compartments would tip the ship forward. When those compartments were filled, water would begin filling the next compartment, then the one after that. Soon, the entire ship would be dragged down.

"How long does the ship have to live?" Smith asked.

Andrews shook his head gravely. "An hour," he replied. "Perhaps a little more."

Captain Smith was staggered. His ship—the unsinkable *Titanic*—was sinking beneath his feet.

And that was not the worst news Captain Smith had to face. He knew that the *Titanic* had a grand total of twenty lifeboats aboard. Those boats had room for a maximum of 1,178 people.

The *Titanic* was carrying over 2,200 people and crew. There was only one thing to do—call for help.

In the wireless office, Jack Phillips had been on duty

for many hours. Engrossed in his work, he had no idea that the *Titanic* had collided with an iceberg. Harold Bride was just waking up to relieve him when both men were surprised by Captain Smith at their door.

"We've struck an iceberg," the captain announced. "You better get ready to send out a call for assistance. But don't send it until I tell you."

With that, Captain Smith left.

Bride and Phillips joked about the situation. The *Titanic* needed to send out a distress call? No one would believe it!

About ten minutes later, the captain returned to the wireless office.

"Send the call for assistance," he ordered.

"What call should I send?" Phillips asked.

"The regulation international call for help," the captain said, and left.

Phillips shrugged his shoulders and began flashing the letters "CQD." "CQ" meant "Stop transmission and pay attention"; "D" meant "distress." He followed with "MGY," the *Titanic*'s call letters. All the while, he and Bride kidded each other about the situation.

A few minutes later, the captain returned to see if they had gotten a response.

"No, sir," Phillips reported.

"Which signal are you sending?" Captain Smith asked.

"CQD, sir."

"I've got an idea," Bride said with a smile. "Send 'SOS.' It's the new distress call. This may be your last chance to send it."

Even Captain Smith chuckled at Bride's joke. Phillips, leaning over the wireless set, clicked out the first "SOS" signal in history.

EIGHT

Sunday, April 14, 1912
11:50 P.M.

"Good night, Mother! Good night, Father!"

Jack Thayer felt good as he buttoned his pajama top. The ocean voyage so far had been a lot of fun. There were lots of activities for him to do. He had met many famous people and made new friends. He was also enjoying the weather. Unlike many of the other passengers, Jack liked the cold, fresh sea air. In fact, he always kept the porthole in his cabin half open, letting a frosty breeze blow through.

As Jack prepared for bed, he noticed something odd: The cold breeze had stopped.

Listening closely, he noticed that the faint hum and

vibrations of the *Titanic*'s engines had stopped, too. The ship had come to a complete halt in mid-ocean. Then, from the open decks, Jack heard voices calling and the sound of distant laughter.

Something was definitely going on.

"I'm going out to see the fun," Jack told his parents. He threw a warm overcoat over his pajamas as he left the cabin.

From the upper first-class decks, Jack could look down onto the forward well deck. It was covered almost ankle deep in chunks of ice that had fallen from the iceberg. Shortly after the collision, a handful of boys from the third-class cabins below had come up on the well deck. There, they horsed around, tossing hunks of ice at each other. Some played a quick game of soccer, kicking a slab of ice back and forth across the deck. They had no idea that something was wrong.

All over the *Titanic,* passengers were noticing that the ship had come to a halt. Few, if any, thought that they were in danger. In the second-class smoking room, the men who had seen the iceberg pass continued their card games.

"I expect the iceberg has scratched off some of the ship's new paint," one man joked. "The captain doesn't like to go on until she is painted up again." The others laughed heartily at the joke.

Another man pointed to the glass of whiskey at his side. "Just run along and see if some ice has come aboard," he said. "I would like some for this."

One of the men in the smoking room was Lawrence Beesley, who had been reading quietly in his cabin when he noticed that the engines had stopped. He had come to the smoking room looking for news. Now, satisfied that things were under control, Beesley left the men to their game. But as he stepped out on the boat deck, he saw several crewmen removing the tarps that covered the lifeboats.

As Beesley took the stairs back down to his cabin on D-deck, he began to realize that things weren't quite right. Not only were the lifeboats being prepared, but the staircase seemed to be tilted slightly forward. What was going on?

Daniel Buckley was fast asleep in his tiny third-class cabin on G-deck when the collision occurred. The sounds of activity in the passage outside the cabin woke him up. Buckley jumped from his warm bunk and instantly knew the ship was in trouble.

His feet had landed in a pool of ice-cold water.

"Get up," Buckley told his cabin mates. "There's something wrong. Water is coming in!"

Buckley's cabin mates laughed.

"Get back into bed," one said. "You're not in Ireland now."

But Buckley, convinced that the ship was in danger, threw on his clothes and left the cramped cabin. Two sailors trotted along the passageway, shouting to the sleeping passengers.

"All up on deck!" they called. "All up on deck, unless you want to get drowned!"

Buckley's heart sank.

The *Titanic*'s passengers had to evacuate the ship.

Buckley did as he was told. He immediately made his way up the stairs to E-deck and headed down the broad corridor leading to the ship's stern, joining the steady stream of other third-class passengers. They were all heading for the back of the ship, as far away as possible from the *Titanic*'s flooded bow. Every one of the passengers had a life jacket in hand.

Life jackets! Buckley had been in such a hurry that he had left his behind.

Buckley turned and began struggling against the tide of people flowing to the back of the ship. He had to get back to his cabin and retrieve his life jacket.

At last, Buckley made it to the stairs. He headed down to F-deck, then turned the corner and started down the stairs to his room on G-deck. Midway down the stairs, Buckley stopped and gasped.

Water covered the bottom three steps. All of G-deck—including his cabin—was already completely underwater. Buckley would have to swim underwater if he wanted to get to his room.

As Buckley watched in horror, the water rose to the top of another step. Then another…then another. Water was steadily climbing the stairs, creeping up to devour them all.

There was no time to lose. Buckley turned and hurried back to the ship's stern.

Near the stern, the other third-class passengers were packed on the landing of the stairs leading to the upper decks. The landing was dim, small, and cramped. Naked lightbulbs sprouted from the low, whitewashed ceiling. Babies and children cried. Groups of people knelt in small circles, praying out loud in a variety of languages.

One of the ship's stewards was patiently trying to tell the passengers to put on their life jackets. Many did not understand him, because they did not speak English. Another steward did his best to translate.

At last, the steward organized a group of women and children to bring to the lifeboats. He led them up the stairs and in the direction of the boat deck, promising to return for another group soon.

One little girl, Anna Sjöblom, did not want to wait for the steward to return. With a friend, she sneaked up the stairs to the rear well deck.

As they stepped into the night air, the two girls breathed deeply. The cold air was a welcome relief after the cramped and stuffy landing. Then Anna shuddered. It was freezing out under the starry sky.

Anna turned to face the maze of steps, ladders, and corridors in front of her. She could see lifeboats being loaded on the boat deck, hundreds of feet away. She knew she *had* to make it up to the lifeboats. Anna and her friend ran up the metal steps to the next deck.

Soon the two girls were hopelessly lost in the *Titanic*'s maze of passages. As third-class passengers, they had never left the rear part of the ship. All they had seen of the *Titanic* was their own plain cabins, the simple third-class dining rooms, and the bare, whitewashed third-class lounge. They had no idea how to get from one part of the ship to another. Every corner they turned led to a dead end. Every door they tried was either locked or led to the staircase of a lower deck.

At last the two girls came across a ladder that led to an upper deck. The large sign draped across the ladder read, "Crew Members Only." Anna turned to her friend and smiled. Determined to find the lifeboats, she pushed the sign away and began to climb.

The top of the ladder disappeared into the shadows. Anna hoped it would take them all the way to the lifeboats on the boat deck.

Suddenly, Anna's friend cried out excitedly.

Anna stopped and looked down. Her friend was staring, wide-eyed, through a porthole. Anna peered through the glass to see what had impressed her so much.

Behind the glass was the first-class dining room. The tables had already been set for breakfast. Anna had never seen anything like it. The tables were covered with embroidered cloths. Even in the dark room, the china plates, crystal juice glasses, and polished silverware shimmered. The walls of the vast room were beautiful, too. They were covered with panels of dark wood and decorated with delicately carved gold swirls.

Anna had heard of such an extraordinary place in fairy tales. But here it was, not far from her plain white room on the ship.

"Let's get a better look," Anna's friend said. "Let's break in!" She cocked her foot, ready to kick in the porthole.

"Don't!" Anna hissed. "Do you want to get us in trouble? If we break the window, the shipping company will make us buy them another one!"

With one last wistful look through the window, Anna and her friend continued up the ladder.

On the boat deck, Anna and her friend joined the crowds gathering around the lifeboats.

* * *

On the second-class deck, Ruth Becker was awakened by shouts and loud footsteps. Nellie Becker stood in the doorway. She asked a steward what the commotion was all about.

"Nothing is the matter," he said reassuringly. "We will be going on in a few minutes."

Mrs. Becker returned to the cabin and calmed her two younger children, who were grumpy and frightened. The four of them sat silently in the cabin, waiting for the reassuring hum of the engines to start up again.

The engines remained silent. There was more shouting from somewhere above deck. Then, suddenly, the quiet was shattered by an earsplitting blast, like a million whistles blaring at once. Ruth put her hands to her ears. The *Titanic*'s engines were blowing off steam.

Mrs. Becker opened the cabin door. Ruth could see people scurrying back and forth in the corridor. Mrs. Becker hailed the steward again.

"What is the trouble?" she asked.

This time, the steward looked at her gravely. "Put your life jackets on immediately and go up to the boat deck," he said.

"Do we have time to dress?" asked Mrs. Becker.

"No, ma'am," he grimly replied. "You have time for nothing."

Ruth and her mother bundled up the smaller children as well as they could and left their cabin. A crowd of passengers trooped along the corridor and up the stairs. Some were fully dressed, while others were still in their pajamas and nightgowns. Like the third-class passengers, they carried bright yellow life jackets.

The Beckers, along with the others, walked up to the boat deck. Ruth was awed by the sight. The night was bitterly cold, but there was no breeze at all. The stars were bright and clear, and it seemed as though you could reach out and touch them. Every electric light on deck burned brightly, making the atmosphere almost festive.

Crowded on the deck were dozens and dozens of passengers. No one seemed panicked. Most people simply milled around, waiting for someone to tell them what to do. Only the constant, earsplitting blare of the steam engines disturbed the tranquil scene.

Ruth watched the crew members bustle about as they carried out their orders. They hurried toward the ship's railings and removed the tarps from another set of lifeboats. Then they used ropes to hoist the boats over the side of the ship.

One man in particular caught Ruth's eye. He wasn't dressed in a uniform, but he seemed to be in charge of the crewmen.

"Hurry! Hurry!" the man yelled, as the crewmen

NINE

Monday, April 15, 1912
12:45 A.M.

"Lifeboats? What do they need of lifeboats?" a woman sarcastically asked the crowd on the boat deck. "This ship could smash a hundred icebergs and not feel it. Ridiculous!"

Most of the *Titanic*'s passengers could not believe what was happening either. They watched more in curiosity than in fear as the crewmen peeled the tarps off the lifeboats and prepared them for launching. How could the *Titanic* be in serious danger? After all, it was an "unsinkable ship"!

On the starboard side of the ship, just opposite the gym, First Officer Murdoch stood alongside Lifeboat

Number 7, the first one ready to launch. In times of crisis, women and children were to be saved first. It was Murdoch's duty to see that the evacuation proceeded smoothly.

"Ladies, this way," he called, pointing to the tiny, frail boat, which hung by ropes over the side of the mighty *Titanic.*

The crowd of passengers warily eyed the boat, then looked down at the cold black sea some sixty feet below. At that moment, the damaged ship seemed safer than the small lifeboats. No one stepped forward to get in.

"Put the brides and grooms in first," someone suggested.

A few pairs of newlyweds, young couples enjoying a honeymoon cruise, cautiously stepped forward. The husbands helped their wives cross the gap between the *Titanic* and the swinging lifeboat. Then they stepped aboard the tiny boat themselves. A handful of other passengers boarded, followed by a few crew members, who would row.

"Are there any more ladies before this boat goes?" First Officer Murdoch called.

None came forward.

"Lower away!" Murdoch shouted.

The boat, made to hold sixty-five people, slowly dropped to the ocean. It was less than half full.

As the lifeboat dropped alongside the *Titanic*'s black

hull, it passed row after row of brightly lit portholes. The passengers huddled together, cold and afraid, as the boat gently settled into the ocean. The sea was as flat and still as a sheet of glass.

"Row for the gangplank door," Murdoch shouted from the boat deck, far above. "Wait there for other passengers!"

The crewmen on Lifeboat Number 7 couldn't hear Murdoch over the constant blare of the steam engines. They immediately began to row away from the *Titanic*.

At the stern of the ship, Quartermaster George Rowe knew that something was wrong. He had seen the iceberg pass dangerously close to the ship, and a number of third-class passengers had asked him what was going on. Rowe could only shrug his shoulders in response. Now, he gasped in surprise as he watched Number 7 row away from the ship.

Quartermaster Rowe decided to find out what was going on. He grabbed the telephone linking him to the ship's bridge. Fourth Officer Joseph Boxhall answered the call.

Rowe identified himself and asked, "Do you know one of the boats is away?"

Fourth Officer Boxhall explained the situation. He told Rowe to come to the bridge right away—and to bring the ship's distress rockets with him.

As a safety precaution, the *Titanic* carried eight distress rockets in a locker at its stern. The bright fireworks exploded with a tremendous boom. They could be seen and heard miles away, and were to be used only as a last resort.

Quartermaster Rowe made his way one deck below to the locker, removed the box of rockets, and headed for the bridge. On the way, he passed through each of the *Titanic*'s passenger areas.

The third-class smoking room was filled with people. Men stood at the bar, trying to order drinks. Someone was playing a piano, and a group of laughing Swedish passengers were doing a ring dance around a crowd of Italians.

Rowe muscled his way through the crowds forming on the rear well deck. As he passed through the second-class corridors, hundreds of confused passengers milled around, wondering what to do.

Up on the boat deck, Rowe saw his fellow crew members hastily preparing the lifeboats. Some were ready to go, but the passengers were still not eager to board the frail wooden boats. Most of them preferred to stay in the enclosed lounge, where it was warm.

The first-class gym was also filled with passengers seeking warmth. Instructor McCawley was proudly showing off the latest pieces of exercise equipment. He encouraged people to try them all. Sitting side by side on a pair of mechanical horses were John Jacob Astor and his lovely young wife. Astor was nonchalantly cutting open a life vest with a knife to show Madeleine what was inside.

On the ship's bridge, Fourth Officer Boxhall and Captain Smith stared intently past the port bow of the ship. Boxhall worked the ship's Morse lamp and flashed a message across the dark ocean. Rowe joined them and followed their gaze.

There, shining faintly on the distant horizon, was a set of lights. It was another ship—no more than ten miles away!

"Fire the rockets!" Captain Smith ordered, hoping that rescue was at hand. "Fire one, and fire another every five or six minutes."

"Aye, aye, Captain."

Rowe began setting up the rockets on the starboard side of the bridge. Captain Smith left them to see how the evacuation of the ship was coming.

A second lifeboat, Number 5, had just been lowered to the sea on the starboard side. It, too, was less than half full. Captain Smith went to the port side of the ship, where more boats were being readied to launch. The crew on that side of the ship were also finding it hard to persuade passengers to leave the seeming safety of the *Titanic*.

Rumors traveled through the crowd: "The *Titanic* is

damaged, but it will certainly stay afloat long enough for another ship to come to its rescue"; "Sending out the lifeboats is just a precaution"; "The poor, freezing people on the lifeboats will come back to the ship first thing in the morning."

The hardest thing for anyone to believe was that the *Titanic* would actually plunge below the water.

Captain Smith watched as Lifeboat Number 6 was lowered from the port side of the ship. Yelling through a megaphone, he told the crewman in charge to row toward the ship he had seen off the port bow.

As Lifeboat Number 6 pulled away from the *Titanic,* the blare of steam escaping from the ship's boilers abruptly stopped. For a few moments, the only sound the frightened people in the lifeboat heard was the lapping of water against oars.

Suddenly, the tinkle of joyful ragtime jazz filled the air. The *Titanic*'s band had made its way to the boat deck. They played upbeat tunes and tried to lift everyone's spirits.

From the lifeboats adrift on the ocean, the *Titanic* looked warm and inviting. Every light on board blazed brightly. Then a sparkling rocket arced into the sky. It exploded with a resounding boom and burst into a brilliant white flower of light, which fell gently down to the smooth surface of the ocean.

The *Titanic* looked like a floating party, but the people on board did not have cause to celebrate. From the lifeboats, the evacuated passengers could see that the rows of brightly lit portholes were no longer parallel to the surface of the water. The ship had tilted forward.

The *Titanic* was sinking headfirst.

TEN

Monday, April 15, 1912
1:00 A.M.

Down in the bowels of the ship, stoker Fred Barrett and two engineers, Jonathan Shepherd and Herbert Harvey, continued to pump water out of the ship's damaged compartments.

Steam swirled in the hot, damp boiler room where they worked. So far, the crewmen had managed to pump the seawater out of the room faster than it came in through the gashed hull. But there was no way of knowing how long they could stay ahead of the water.

The bulkhead in front of them groaned and creaked ominously. The boiler room on the other side was already filled with water.

Even if they could not save the ship, the men knew it was important to keep the water out as long as possible. When the flooding water made its way to the electric turbines near the stern, the ship would lose its electric power. That meant no more lights—and, more important, no more wireless radio communication.

Suddenly, Engineer Shepherd stepped into an open manhole and screamed out in pain. Harvey and Barrett peered through the dark and steam and saw him lying on the deck, writhing in agony. They rushed to his side.

"His leg is broken," Harvey said, as he and Barrett dragged Shepherd into the next boiler room.

"I'll be all right," Shepherd insisted, grimacing. "Just keep those pumps going!"

Barrett and Harvey returned to their stations.

Just then, an immense wave of water exploded into the boiler room. The forward bulkhead had disintegrated. The "watertight" compartment had blown up under the intense pressure.

Harvey rushed to Shepherd's side.

"Save yourself!" Harvey called to Barrett.

Barrett instinctively scrambled up the first few rungs of the escape ladder, then stopped and looked down as Harvey struggled to help Shepherd to his feet. Barrett was about to climb down to help when the two men disappeared under the churning, foamy water.

There was nothing Barrett could do but climb up the ladder to the boat deck.

Far above, in the wireless office, Jack Phillips continued sending distress signals. So far he had gotten through to the *Frankfurt,* a steamer almost 200 miles away. The *Olympic*—the *Titanic*'s sister ship, which was on its way to England—also responded. But the *Olympic* was 500 miles away. It could not reach the *Titanic* before the following night.

As he was about to send another SOS, Phillips got a clear, strong message. It was from the ship *Carpathia,* whose wireless operator had just turned on his set.

"Come at once," Phillips immediately responded. "We have struck a berg. It's a CQD, old man."

It was a few seconds before Phillips got a response. Shocked by the news, the *Carpathia*'s wireless operator asked whether he should tell his captain.

"Yes! *Quick!*" Phillips pleaded.

Minutes later, Phillips received another message: The *Carpathia* was on its way to help.

Phillips asked Harold Bride to tell Captain Smith the good news: The smaller ship was only fifty-eight miles away.

Bride made his way through the *Titanic*'s crowded boat deck. The decks were tilted forward at a dangerously sharp angle, but he managed to find the captain and tell him that the *Carpathia* was on its way to rescue them.

At first, Captain Smith was overjoyed. But then he did some quick calculations. Even at full steam, it would take the *Carpathia* four hours to reach the *Titanic*. Four hours from now would be too late.

Bride returned to the wireless office, shivering from the cold. Phillips glanced up from the desk.

"Put some clothes on," he said. "You'll need them."

Bride looked down, embarrassed. In all the excitement, he had forgotten he was still in his pajamas.

Phillips continued to tap out the SOS call. He noticed that his wireless signal was growing weaker; just then, Captain Smith appeared at the office doorway.

"Tell the *Carpathia* to come as quickly as possible," Captain Smith said grimly. "The engine rooms are taking water. We can't last much longer."

"Aye, aye, Captain."

Phillips continued working the wireless set; Bride silently draped a coat around his partner's shoulders.

Outside, they could hear the faint gurgling of water as the *Titanic*'s bow dipped lower and lower into the sea.

Up on the boat deck, the crew continued loading the lifeboats with women and children. As Lifeboat Number 8 filled with passengers, an elderly couple, Isidor and Ida Straus, said their final good-byes. Then, with one foot in the lifeboat, Mrs. Straus changed her mind.

"We have been living together for many years," she said, taking her husband's hand. "Where you go, I go."

With that, Mrs. Straus stepped back onto the *Titanic*.

People on deck, shocked, urged her to get on the boat.

"No!" she said. "I will not be separated from my husband."

The elderly couple firmly held hands. "As we have lived, so will we die. Together."

Isidor and Ida Straus then sat side by side in deck chairs. They listened to the music and watched the crowds fill the lifeboats.

Lifeboat Number 8 was lowered to the ocean. Then the crowds surged to the back part of the boat deck, where the other boats were being filled.

There was still one small lifeboat left at the front of the boat deck, Emergency Boat Number 1. First Officer Murdoch was in charge of loading it. Unfortunately, not many passengers were nearby.

"Excuse me, may we get in the boat?" asked a well-dressed gentleman.

"Yes, I wish you would," Murdoch replied.

The man, British nobleman Sir Cosmo Duff-Gordon, climbed aboard. He helped both his wife, Lucile, and her secretary climb over the rail into the tiny boat.

The only other passengers near Emergency Boat Number 1 were two men traveling first class.

"Jump in!" Murdoch yelled at them.

One of the men managed to scramble on board the tiny boat. The other one leaned over the rail and rolled head over heels onto the emergency boat's floor.

First Officer Murdoch laughed out loud. "That's the funniest thing I've seen all night!" he exclaimed.

Murdoch ordered some crew members into the boat to row.

"Stand off to the ship's side, then return when we call you," he told the men.

Emergency Boat Number 1 was lowered to the ocean. It was designed to hold forty people. It held exactly twelve.

As the lifeboat slowly pulled away, its passengers looked back at the magnificent *Titanic*. They were shocked to see how much it had sunk. On the bow of the ship, the *Titanic*'s name was now just above the waterline.

ELEVEN

Monday, April 15, 1912
1:12 A.M.

Ruth Becker waited patiently with her mother and two siblings on the A-deck promenade. It was almost their turn to board the lifeboats.

The *Titanic*'s crew was lowering some of the lifeboats until they were even with A-deck. There, women and children would crawl through the windows into the small boats. By now, the crew had no trouble finding passengers willing to leave the ship. Women and children crowded around the windows as crewmen hastily helped them out and into the open boats.

Ruth watched as some seventy people filled Lifeboat Number 11. When the boat was so full that it seemed likely to tip over, a crewman reached over, grabbed Ruth's sister, Marion, and tossed her aboard. Another crewman snatched Ruth's baby brother, Richard, from their mother and handed him to a woman onboard.

"My children!" Mrs. Becker screamed. "Oh, please let me go with my children!"

"All right, but you're the last!" said a crewman, helping Mrs. Becker through the window. "Lower away!" he called to the men on the boat deck above.

Then, as Lifeboat Number 11 headed down alongside the *Titanic*, Mrs. Becker saw Ruth, still standing on A-deck.

"Ruth!" she screamed as the boat disappeared into the night. "Ruth! Get on the next boat!"

Ruth looked down the promenade to where a crewman stood by an open window. Through it, Ruth could see a crowded boat swinging on ropes.

"Any more women?" the crewman called out.

Ruth calmly walked up to the man.

"May I get on board?" she asked.

Without a word, the man lifted Ruth up and hoisted her through the window. She tumbled into Lifeboat Number 13, which rocked back and forth under her weight.

Ruth looked around her. It took a few moments for her eyes to adjust to the darkness in the boat. Then she saw that the lifeboat was filled with people, mostly frightened women and children, who sat trembling in the cold.

At the helm of the tiny boat sat a man wearing just a soaking wet T-shirt and trousers. He looked utterly exhausted. It was stoker Fred Barrett, who'd been put in charge of Lifeboat Number 13 as soon as he made it to the boat deck.

"Is that all?" called a voice from overhead.

"Wait! There's two more!" a voice from A-deck replied, as two more women crawled through the window and into the boat.

"Lower away!" called the voice from above.

"No!" screamed a woman from the boat deck. "Stop!"

A crewman stuck his head over the rail.

"Here, someone, catch!" he called—and tossed a bundle into the boat. One of the crewmen on board caught the bundle, which was wrapped in a blanket. The man unwrapped it to find a gurgling baby. Ruth watched as a young couple scrambled over the boat deck rail and jumped into the lifeboat, barely escaping the *Titanic* with their baby.

"Lower away!" came the call from above. Then, with the squeak of ropes and pulleys, Lifeboat Number 13 began to descend into the darkness.

Two sets of crewmen manned the ropes at the bow and stern of the lifeboat. Though they tried to lower the boat evenly, first the bow would drop down and then they'd lower the stern too fast. As the boat moved down alongside the ship, Ruth was certain that they would tip over. At last, the crew managed to lower both ends at the same time. The lifeboat dropped, jerkily, down to the sea.

Peering over the side, Ruth saw a huge stream of rushing water pour from the side of the *Titanic*. Their boat was being lowered directly into it!

"Take care, lads, or she'll be swamped," called Barrett, sitting at the helm. "Use the oars!"

The men on board unlashed the oars and held them over the side of the boat. As they neared the stream of water, the men used the oars to push off from the side of the *Titanic*. It worked! The rush of water thrust Lifeboat Number 13 alongside the huge ship.

The little lifeboat drifted swiftly along on the current—then stopped with a jerk. The ropes that had lowered it to the sea were still attached. The crewmen, unused to the lifeboat, tried to figure out how to release the ropes.

In the water, Lifeboat Number 13 seemed dangerously unsteady after the solid decks of the *Titanic*. As she tried to adjust to the bobbing of the lifeboat, Ruth glanced wistfully up at the big ship. She gasped. Another lifeboat—Number 15—was being lowered right on top of them! Ruth watched in terror as the crewmen in her boat struggled to cut the ropes that still held them to the *Titanic*.

Lower and lower, the other boat dropped. Ruth and the others shrieked to the sailors on the *Titanic* to stop lowering the other lifeboat. But they did not hear the cries.

Two of the men in Lifeboat Number 13 stood up as the boat above got closer and closer. They placed their hands on the underside of Number 15 and desperately tried to push their own boat out. Ruth ducked down and clenched her eyes shut. She was sure the people in Number 13 would be crushed any second. If only she had stayed on board the *Titanic*!

At the last moment, Barrett managed to cut the ropes. Lifeboat Number 13 drifted away as Number 15 splashed into the water behind it.

Ruth sighed with relief as the crewmen rowed their boat away from the *Titanic*. She looked back at the ship, still brightly lit against the star-filled sky. Hundreds and hundreds of faces lined the rails of the *Titanic*'s decks, watching as their boat slowly moved away.

Ruth shuddered as a terrible thought crossed her mind. There were no other lifeboats that she could see. If the *Titanic* really were to sink, what would happen to all the poor souls still on board?

TWELVE

"Let us through! Let us through!"

Daniel Buckley stood on the boat deck with a crowd of other third-class passengers and rattled the locked metal gate in front of him. A few women and children had already been taken to lifeboats, but the rest of the third-class passengers had been told to wait. Now, everyone was restless and growing more and more alarmed. They worried that the first- and second-class passengers would be evacuated first, and that when it was their turn no lifeboats would be left.

On the other side of the gate, a steward shook his head.

"This is a second-class deck," he said, sneering. "The likes of you have to stay in third class!"

One of the men next to Buckley, a huge fellow, bellowed with rage and threw his body against the gate. It began to give. Once more, he rammed his shoulder against the gate. It broke away.

"Just wait till I get my hands on you!" the man yelled as he trampled over the gate. The steward scurried away.

Buckley and the others weren't interested in revenge. They ran through the gateway and scrambled up the stairs to the boat deck, where the last lifeboats were being loaded.

Almost two hours had passed since the *Titanic* had scraped the iceberg. The ship was tilted forward and to port. Everyone aboard knew the *Titanic* was in trouble.

Still, many people clung to the hope that they were not in serious danger. After all, the lights were still burning brightly, and the band continued to play happy, upbeat tunes. A rumor made the rounds: The *Titanic* could stay afloat for at least another eight hours. By that time, the *Carpathia* or the *Olympic* would arrive. Everyone on the *Titanic* would be saved.

On A-deck near the bridge, crewmen began loading Lifeboat Number 4. The *Titanic* was listing so badly that a gap had opened between the lifeboat and the ship's side. The crew placed deck chairs across the gap so that passengers could crawl into the small boat.

Among the passengers in Lifeboat Number 4 was nineteen-year-old Madeleine Astor. Her husband, John Jacob Astor, watched with concern as his bride sat in the rocking boat.

"May I accompany my wife?" he asked Second Officer Lightoller, who was in charge of loading Number 4. "I want to protect her. She is pregnant, you know."

Lightoller shook his head.

"No, sir," he said. "No men are allowed in these boats until women are loaded first."

He continued helping women passengers, and the boat was quickly filled.

"What boat is this?" Astor asked Lightoller.

"Number Four, sir," Lightoller replied.

Astor nodded. He wanted to remember which boat his wife was in, so that he could find her in the morning.

"Take care of yourself, my dear." Astor removed his gloves and tossed them to his wife. "I'll see you soon!" he called as the boat was lowered to the sea.

The passengers on board Lifeboat Number 4 were shocked at how quickly they reached the surface of the sea. They saw water pouring through the portholes on C-deck. The entire bow of the *Titanic* was now submerged. The sea glowed an eerie, murky green, as lights shone through the portholes under water.

"What are your orders?" a woman passenger asked the seaman in charge of the boat.

"There is a companionway aft, and we are ordered to go there," he replied.

The companionways were large doors used to load the ship. Lifeboat Number 4 was supposed to pick up more passengers there.

Many people on the boat wanted to get away from the *Titanic* as quickly as possible. But the crew followed orders and rowed alongside the ship toward its stern. From within the hull came the tinkling sounds of glass breaking. As the ship's tilt grew steeper, plates and glasses slid off tables and shattered on the steel decks.

When Lifeboat Number 4 neared the stern of the *Titanic,* two men dropped from a deck overhead. One landed in the bow, almost capsizing the boat. The other man splashed into the water next to the boat. The women aboard helped pull him in.

There were no open companionways to be seen, so the lifeboat crew began rowing away. As the boat cleared the *Titanic*'s stern, the passengers gasped. The great ship tipped forward. Its three propellers, each the size of a windmill, slowly emerged from the sea and hung, dripping, over the calm, flat water.

Oarsmen in the lifeboats rowed furiously away from the *Titanic,* toward the lights of the ship seen off its port bow. If the ship was going to sink, they did not want to be nearby. They feared that as the *Titanic* went down, it would drag them along with it.

But soon the distant lights were gone. The ship Captain Smith had seen had disappeared into the night. It had ignored the *Titanic*'s distress rockets.

People still on the *Titanic* started to panic, as they realized that the last of the lifeboats were being loaded and launched. Fifth Officer Harold Lowe, in charge of loading the third-to-last, noticed a teenaged boy in the boat.

"Get out," Lowe ordered. "This boat is for women and children."

"Please let me stay," the teenager pleaded. "I don't want to die!"

Lowe pulled a revolver from his belt. "I give you just ten seconds to get back on that ship before I blow your brains out!" he threatened.

"No! No! Let me stay!"

"For God's sake, be a man."

A little girl, sobbing, grabbed Lowe by the arm. "Oh, Mr. Man," she said, "please don't shoot the poor man."

At last, the teenager scrambled from the boat back onto the deck of the *Titanic*.

Lowe looked over the crowd of people sitting in the lifeboat—more than fifty women and children. One person, huddling under a black shawl, looked suspiciously large. Lowe reached down and peeled away the shawl. The passenger was a man trying to stow away on the lifeboat. Lowe roughly grabbed him and threw him back onto the *Titanic*.

There were no officers on board the lifeboat, so Lowe took command. As he stood in the frail vessel, he worried that it had been overloaded. The boat swung heavily from the davits. It seemed likely to collapse before it could reach the water.

"Do you think the boat will make it?" Lowe asked a crewmen.

"She's hanging all right," he replied.

"Then lower away," Lowe ordered.

The lifeboat began to drop to the water. As it passed the open decks beneath the boat deck, Lowe saw crowds of men standing at the rails, about to jump aboard.

"Don't try it!" Lowe yelled, sure the boat would collapse if even one more person got on board. As the men threw their legs over the rails, he pulled his gun and fired. The men jumped back.

As the lifeboat neared the water, it began to tip dangerously, bow first, until it was nearly spilling its passengers into the water.

The seaman sitting at the tiller pulled his knife, turned around, and cut the rope holding the stern. The boat dropped five feet, hitting the water with a thud and a splash. A number of those on board screamed.

On the *Titanic,* crewmen prepared to load the last two lifeboats still hanging on the davits. These boats were called collapsibles, because their sides were made of sturdy canvas, not wood.

On the starboard side of the ship, purser Herbert McElroy took charge of loading Collapsible Boat C. A number of men scrambled into the small boat, pushing aside women and children. McElroy yelled at the men to get out and fired his gun into the air. The men crawled out of Collapsible C, and the woman and children climbed on board. Within minutes, the boat was filled.

"Any more women?" McElroy called.

There were none.

"Lower away!" McElroy called, and the boat began to drop.

As Collapsible Boat C disappeared below the rails, two men quietly slipped aboard. One was William Carter, whose family had left a few minutes before on another boat.

The other man was Bruce Ismay, head of the White Star Line.

On the other side of the ship, Chief Officer Henry Wilde and Second Officer Lightoller took charge of loading Collapsible D, the last boat hanging from the ship's davits. Looking over the canvas sides of the collapsible, Lightoller found a number of men huddled under its benches.

"Get out!" Lightoller ordered.

The men didn't budge. Lightoller pulled his gun.

"Don't make me use this!" he barked.

The men sheepishly left. Wilde ordered the crewmen nearby to lock arms and form a ring around the boat. They were to let only women and children through.

Within minutes, the boat was filled. Wilde looked over the people on board. There were no officers in Collapsible D. He turned to his shipmate.

"You go with her, Lightoller," Wilde said.

Instead, Lightoller jumped to the ropes, ready to lower the boat to the water. He refused to leave the ship when there were still women and children aboard.

ꟼHIRTEEN

After the last of the lifeboats left the *Titanic,* an eerie quiet came over the ship. But Chief Baker Charles Joughin was keeping busy. He walked up and down the now empty promenade on A-deck, grabbing deck chairs and throwing them off the ship. The chairs splashed loudly in the water below.

When the time came, the floating chairs would give the *Titanic*'s survivors something to grab onto.

"It won't be long now," Joughin muttered to himself as the tilting deck lurched beneath his feet. Around him, the bright electric lights began to buzz slightly as they dimmed and burned red.

Joughin headed "uphill," toward the stern of the *Titanic*. It would be the last part of the ship to go under.

Up on the boat deck, Jack Thayer felt strangely calm. He watched as a group of crewmen struggled to unlash a pair of collapsible boats stowed on the roof of the officers' quarters. The deck was pitching forward so steeply that it was next to impossible to free the two boats.

Jack stood quietly chatting with a friend, Milton Long, as throngs of people streamed past them to the stern of the ship. Behind Jack and Milton, the band had stopped performing upbeat tunes; now they played quiet, mournful hymns.

"The deck is getting steeper," Milton said.

"It is," Jack agreed.

He looked out over the water. A few hundred yards away, he could see half-empty lifeboats dotting the sea. Jack had seen his mother get into one of the boats. He prayed that his father had made it onto one of them, too.

"What do you say we make a swim for it?" Jack suggested, nodding toward the boats. "The boats aren't that far, and many of them have plenty of room."

Milton looked down at the black, frigid water and grimaced. "I can't swim," he said sheepishly. He looked back at the band, which had just started a new song. "I still can't believe she'll sink," he said, shaking his head. "What do you say we take our chances on the *Titanic*?"

Jack smiled briefly, then patted his friend on the shoulder. "Sure thing," he said. "We'll stick together, no matter what."

In the wireless office, Jack Phillips continued sending out a very weak distress call. Harold Bride draped a life jacket over his partner's shoulders. Phillips didn't even look up.

"Men, you have done your full duty," a tired voice said.

Bride turned, startled. Captain Smith stood at the door of the wireless office.

"You can do no more," the captain continued. "Abandon your cabin. Now it's every man for himself. That's the way of it at this kind of time. Every man for himself."

With that, the captain left.

Bride went to the door and looked out. Water was creeping up the boat deck. Hearing voices overhead, he peered up at the roof above, where the crewmen were desperately trying to free the last two collapsibles.

Inside the wireless office, Phillips continued tapping out the distress call. He was hoping for a miracle: that some nearby ship would hear their call and come before it was too late.

"You heard the captain," Bride said, returning to the office. "We should clear out while we can."

Bride ducked behind the curtain separating their bunk

from the wireless office. When he turned back, he saw a large, rough-looking man leaning over Phillips—trying to steal the life jacket off Phillips's back!

"Stop!" Bride yelled, jumping on the man.

The man shoved Bride away and turned back to Phillips, who had finally thrown aside his headset. Phillips and the man wrestled. The thief tried desperately to get the life jacket, but Bride jumped back to his feet and grabbed him from behind, pinning his arms. Phillips punched the thief, who slumped over, unconscious.

"Come on!" Phillips panted, out of breath. "Let's clear out!"

The two wireless operators rushed from the cabin as ice-cold water trickled onto the deck.

"Phillips! This way!" Bride yelled, pointing to the two lifeboats on the roof of the officers' quarters.

He watched, torn, as his partner rushed away from him and toward the stern of the ship. Phillips disappeared in the crowd. That was the last Bride ever saw of him.

Bride scrambled up on the roof of the officers' quarters, where the crewmen were using knives to cut the ropes holding the boat to the roof.

"There! It's free!" someone called out.

"Lower it to the deck! We'll float it off the boat!"

"How? It's too bloody steep!"

"Let's use the oars," one man suggested. "Prop them

from the deck to the roof. We can slide the boat down with them."

The men scrambled to set up the oars as the *Titanic* tilted forward. People screamed in terror as the stern of the ship rose higher and higher from the water.

The crewmen tried lowering the boat down the oars, but the angle was too steep. They lost their grip and the boat crashed to the deck below. Bride jumped from the roof and grabbed one of the boat's oarlocks.

At that moment, the *Titanic* lurched forward. The ship tilted forward at a crazy angle, and the tiny collapsible boat slid down the deck with Bride, hanging on, dragged behind it.

The last thing Bride saw was Captain Smith standing at the edge of the boat deck. The bearded old man took one last look around, then dived into the sea.

In the next second, Bride was engulfed in the icy sea.

The water temperature was only twenty-eight degrees Fahrenheit, and when he came to the surface, his entire body was numb. Bride looked around wildly. The sky was pitch-black. He could hear his breathing echo loudly off the water's surface. The night was as dark as a grave.

Where are the stars? he wondered.

His heart began to pound in panic.

Am I already dead?

Then, suddenly, Bride realized that he was trapped *under* the lifeboat.

Bride took a deep breath and closed his eyes. He tucked his body and plunged into the frigid water, kicking wildly, desperately trying to pull himself down. Bride swam until he thought he was clear of the boat. Then he stopped kicking and let his life jacket pull him up.

As his head broke the surface, Bride blew water from his nose and mouth. He shook the water from his face. The overturned boat was floating a few feet away. Bride swam to it and managed to pull himself on. Exhausted, he lay silent for a few minutes, panting, in the cold night air.

¢OURTEEN

Monday, April 15, 1912
2:20 A.M.

A huge wave rolled up the boat deck as the *Titanic* pitched forward.

Jack Thayer clung desperately to the rail. He watched in horror as hundreds of people rushed up the deck, struggling to stay ahead of the wave. Most of them were washed under.

"Let's go!" Jack called to his friend Milton.

"All right!" Milton threw his leg over the rails and stood there, holding on.

The two young men could not wait any longer. They had to jump ship or risk being trapped in the *Titanic* when it went down.

Jack straddled the rail. The two men shook hands.

"You are coming, aren't you, boy?" Milton asked, terror in his eyes.

"I'm with you," Jack said, unbuttoning his coat.

Milton let go of the rail and slid down the side of the *Titanic*. He hit the water and was immediately swept up in a torrent pouring through the windows of A-deck. Milton had been sucked back into the ship!

Jack stood at the rail. He closed his eyes, gathered his courage, and jumped as far as he could from the *Titanic*.

The icy water stabbed Jack like a thousand knives as he plunged beneath the surface. He kicked furiously and at last emerged, gulping air, treading water, desperately trying to breathe. At last, when he had gathered his wits, Jack swam for his life, heading away from the *Titanic*.

After a few moments, he turned around in the water—and gasped at what he saw.

The *Titanic* was about forty yards away. It stood out, still brightly lit, against the starry night sky. The stern of the great ship rose higher and higher above the water, as hundreds of people, screaming in terror, scrambled as far astern as possible. Dozens and dozens of them slid down the deck and were swallowed up by the water. Those who managed to hang on looked like swarming bees as they clung to the rails of the great ship. They dropped, singly and in groups, from the decks of the *Titanic*.

Then came a low, thundering *boom* from deep inside the ship. A shower of sparks and soot spurted from the first smokestack. Jack watched in horror as the smokestack tore free and shot forward like a missile. It slammed into the ocean, crushing dozens of people who struggled in the water beneath it.

The funnel's impact made a huge wave roll away from the *Titanic*. The wave engulfed Jack and carried him farther from the doomed ship. When he came to the surface at last and shook the stinging salt water from his face, Jack could hardly believe his eyes: A few feet away from him was an overturned lifeboat.

With a few powerful kicks, Jack made it to the boat. He crawled onto it and turned to watch the *Titanic*'s last awful moments.

The huge ship was now doing a headstand, its massive stern sticking hundreds of feet straight out of the water. Miraculously, the lights still burned. Suddenly, they blinked and went out—then flashed back on for a second.

And then the *Titanic* fell dark.

Boom! Boom! Boom! Boom!

A vast, deep, low sound rumbled over the surface of the water. The ship's heavy machinery and cargo had come loose and were dropping to the bow of the *Titanic*. The three engines, the twenty-nine boilers, dozens of cars in storage, all the luggage, thousands of plates, glasses—

everything on board the ship plunged forward.

The booming faded, only to be replaced by the screams of the hundreds of passengers and crew members who still managed to cling to the deck. The ship hung in the same vertical position for what seemed an eternity.

Jack watched in awe, too fascinated to be afraid. The dark ship loomed high above, like a giant black finger pointing into the star-filled sky.

Then— *C-c-c-crack! Crack! Crack!*

With a series of sharp metallic sounds, the *Titanic* split in two. The water-filled bow knifed down, plunging into the abyss.

The stern settled back for a few seconds, then began to tip forward. More screaming people dropped from it into the freezing water below. The stern continued to rise, until it stood almost straight up.

Charles Joughin was one of a handful of men standing on the back end of the ship. The mammoth rudder and giant propellers glistened in the starlight before them. Beneath their feet were the painted words "R.M.S. *Titanic.*" Behind them, the British flag hung limply from the ship's flagpole.

From all around came the screams of people clinging to the ship's rails or freezing in the water below.

"She's floating!" one of the men called.

"She's going to float!"

The *Titanic* hung in this upright position for a few more minutes. Then the men standing on the ship's stern felt a slight shudder and rumble beneath their feet. The hulk of the *Titanic* began to twist. One of the men lost his balance and fell, screaming, into the water.

The *Titanic* slowly began its final dive.

"Let's jump for it!"

One by one, the men leaped off the stern of the ship, splashing into the water below.

The stern was dropping, slowly, straight into the sea. Joughin felt as though he were riding down an elevator. He kept his balance as the mighty *Titanic* made its final plunge.

Then, just as the water washed over the stern, Joughin stepped away from the ship and began to tread water. The flagpole behind him disappeared beneath the surface with a faint gurgle.

The *Titanic* was gone.

Charles Joughin was the last man off the ship. He left the sinking *Titanic* without even getting his hair wet.

¢IFTEEN

Monday, April 15, 1912
2:25 A.M.

The surface of the water was littered with wreckage—
floating chairs, hunks of cork from within the bulkheads,
and empty life jackets. But the *Titanic* was nowhere to be
seen.

Jack Thayer, Harold Bride, Second Officer Lightoller,
and twenty other men had managed to get to the overturned lifeboat. They clung to it for dear life.

"Where's she at?" someone quietly asked.

"Who?" a voice muttered.

"The *Titanic*!"

"She's gone," the voice replied. "She's gone forever."

A few more men swam up and climbed aboard. The

boat began to rock in the water. Then, with a loud *gulp,* a pocket of air escaped from beneath, and the small craft dipped dangerously low in the water.

"Is there room aboard?" a familiar voice called from the darkness.

"No!" one of the men yelled.

"Hold on to what you have, old boy," another voice said. "One more of you would sink us all."

"All right, boys," the swimmer replied. "Good luck, and God bless you."

With that, he disappeared into the dark night.

"Blimey," one of the men on the boat said. "You know who that was, don't you?"

"Who?"

"It was Captain Smith. I swear it was!"

Then the men fell silent.

Across the water came a sound that reminded Jack Thayer of locusts chirping on a quiet summer night. But this sound filled him with horror. It was the sound of more than a thousand people crying desperately for help as they slowly froze to death in the icy water.

Harold Bride put his hands to his ears, trying to block out the sound. But he couldn't. He was too exhausted to weep, although he felt as though his heart would break. Then, just when he thought he could stand it no more, a reassuring voice broke in on his dark thoughts.

"I say, men," Second Officer Lightoller declared, "don't you think we ought to pray?"

The men on the overturned boat recited the Lord's Prayer.

The people in the other lifeboats had rowed far from the *Titanic,* fearing that the ship would drag their tiny boats down with it. Now that the ship was gone, the survivors debated whether or not to row back to save some of their shipmates.

Lifeboat Number 4, with Madeleine Astor aboard, rowed the hundreds of yards back to the others. It took almost a half an hour to reach the spot where the *Titanic* had gone down. By that time, they found only five people still alive. After being pulled aboard the lifeboat, four of the people passed out. Two of them never woke up.

Most of the passengers in Lifeboat Number 6 wanted to try to save others. But Quartermaster Robert Hichens, at the tiller, refused to go.

"Those drowning men would capsize this boat in a second," he said. "What's the point of going back for a lot of stiffs?"

Hichens got his way.

Lifeboat Number 1 held only twelve survivors. They had room for at least twenty-eight more. But when the crewman in charge suggested going back, Lady Lucile

Duff-Gordon said they should not. She was afraid they would be swamped. The crewman did not try to argue with the wife of a nobleman. They sat silently as the distant cries died away.

Lady Duff-Gordon gazed out at the water and put her arm around the shoulder of her secretary, Laura Francatelli.

"There is your beautiful nightdress, gone," she sighed.

"Never mind your nightdress, madam, as long as you have your life," one of the crewmen snapped.

He turned to Sir Cosmo Duff-Gordon.

"I suppose you have lost everything?" he asked.

"Of course," Sir Cosmo said.

"But you can get some more?"

"Yes," Sir Cosmo admitted.

"Well, we've lost all our kit and the company won't give us any more," the man said. "And what is more, our pay stops from tonight!"

As soon as the ship went down, the seamen had lost their jobs.

"You fellows don't need to worry about that," Sir Cosmo said. "I'll give you five pounds each to start a new kit."

Of all the officers in lifeboats, Fifth Officer Lowe, in charge of Lifeboat Number 14, showed the most ability. He gathered five of the lifeboats and lashed them togeth-

er. Some of the boats, like Number 14, were full of survivors. Others were barely half full. Lowe ordered the
passengers to shift from boat to boat, until they were
evenly distributed. Then he and a few other crewmen
rowed an empty boat back to look for survivors.

They found a grisly scene. Dead bodies, held up by life
jackets, clogged the water. The men found it hard to row,
because the water was so thick with corpses. Lowe and
the others found only four people still alive. One of those
survivors died before the night was over.

Meanwhile, the men on the overturned lifeboat were fac-
ing a crisis. As the long night wore on, their boat sank
lower in the water. Soon the men had to stand on the
boat, as the icy water crept up their pant legs.

Officer Lightoller took charge. He organized the
men to stand in two rows. Then, as the boat shifted one
way or the other, he ordered the men to lean in the
opposite direction. This enabled the swamped boat to
stay afloat.

As morning drew near, the still water began to grow
choppy. The men on the overturned boat found it harder
and harder to keep their balance. Two of them collapsed
into the water and floated away.

Bride lifted the spirits of those who remained by
telling them that the *Carpathia* was on its way and would

be along by morning. Lightoller scanned the southern horizon, hoping to see a sign of the rescue ship.

Then, just as the first rays of dawn lightened the eastern sky, he saw a faint glow on the horizon, followed by a distant *boom*.

It was a rocket! The *Carpathia* was nearby, firing its rockets to alert the *Titanic*'s survivors.

Unfortunately, the *Carpathia* was still a long way off. The men standing on the boat were not sure they could last until it arrived. The water was growing choppier, and their boat was sinking lower and lower. Already the water was up to their waists.

Off to the side, Lightoller saw another sight that made his heart race. It was the string of lifeboats Fifth Officer Lowe had organized. Lightoller fished his officer's whistle from his pocket and blew it.

"Come over and take us off!" he yelled.

The people in the other boats could hardly believe their eyes. It looked as if a group of men were standing on one of the *Titanic*'s funnels!

One of the lifeboats, Number 12, separated from the others and rowed over to the overturned collapsible. The freezing men managed to move from their swamped boat to Number 12. After they all got on board, Number 12 was loaded with more than seventy-five people. It rode so low in the water that waves splashed over the side.

Under Lightoller's command, the boat headed for the *Carpathia*.

By now, the sun was almost up. It was the dawn of a cold, beautiful day.

As the survivors of the *Titanic* peered around them, they saw that they were not alone. The water was covered with large, jagged, snow-white icebergs. They reflected the rising sun in brilliant pink and blue.

"Oh, look, Mother," said one child in a lifeboat rowing to the *Carpathia*.

He pointed to a radiant, deadly iceberg.

"Look at the beautiful North Pole...with no Santa Claus on it."

SIXTEEN

Monday, April 15, 1912
8:30 A.M.

Harold Bride felt something he'd never expected to feel again. He felt warm.

Bride sat huddled under a blanket in one of the *Carpathia*'s lounges. The ship seemed small and frail after the mighty *Titanic*. But at least it was dry and warm. Bride was overjoyed to be aboard. So were the rest of the hundreds of *Titanic* survivors jamming the *Carpathia*'s lounges and decks.

Both Bride's feet were swollen and purple, and one of them was totally numb. The *Carpathia*'s doctor told him that he had frostbite.

It could have been worse, Bride thought. The image of

Jack Phillips rushing to the ship's stern came to his mind. Bride blinked back a tear. *Yes, it could have been a lot worse.*

"Excuse me, young man…" a soft voice interrupted.

Bride looked up to see one of the *Carpathia*'s officers standing in front of him.

"Excuse me," the officer repeated. "Weren't you one of the *Titanic*'s wireless officers?"

"That's right, sir," Bride replied.

The officer looked embarrassed.

"I'm not quite sure how to ask you this, not after what you've been through…" He smiled awkwardly. "We have more than six hundred *Titanic* survivors aboard. Each one wants to send word to their loved ones to let them know that they're safe. Our poor wireless officer doesn't quite know what's hit him…"

"You need help," Bride said.

"If you don't mind too terribly much."

Bride struggled to his feet and snatched his crutches from the wall.

"It's all right," Bride said, hobbling along after the officer. "It's my duty. I always do my duty."

Bride nobly followed the officer to the *Carpathia*'s wireless office and began tapping out hundreds of messages.

All of America, including the managers of the White Star Line, was stunned to learn about the *Titanic*. No one had dreamed that such a tragedy could happen to the "unsinkable ship." In fact, several newspapers, such as *The Wall Street Journal*, had reported exactly the opposite. They claimed that the *Titanic* had not sunk—and that everyone survived.

On the *Carpathia*, the *Titanic*'s stunned survivors sobbed openly. Many wept with happiness when they found out that their loved ones were safe.

Ruth Becker met her family in a tearful reunion. Nellie Becker had been terrified all night, thinking that Ruth had gone down with the *Titanic*.

Jack Thayer and his mother, overjoyed to see each other, spent the next hours searching the *Carpathia* for Mr. Thayer. Their tears of joy became tears of sadness: They did not find him.

Throughout the ship, *Titanic* survivors felt the deepest grief imaginable. Most of them had lost someone—a husband, a parent, a friend—when the *Titanic* sank. In fact, the *Carpathia* would forever after be known as the "ship of widows."

As the rescue ship steamed back to New York, the fine spring weather turned bad. A storm rocked the small vessel, and the passengers huddled together in crowded, cramped cabins. Many watched in terror as rain lashed the portholes and the boat swayed unsteadily on the waves.

As the *Carpathia* weathered the storm, a group of survivors gathered in the dining room with the *Titanic*'s remaining officers. Second Officer Lightoller was the highest-ranking crewman to survive.

"Officer Lightoller, an ugly rumor is going about," one passenger said. "Some people are saying that the *Titanic* was warned that there was ice ahead. They say Captain Smith knew we were entering dangerous waters, and he did nothing to prevent the accident. Surely that's not true, is it?"

Officer Lightoller said nothing. He gazed at the pale, agonized faces around him.

"It is true we received ice warnings," Lightoller at last admitted.

The crowded room fell into a stunned silence. Then a few passengers began to sob quietly. All were filled with horror and despair.

The world's greatest ship had plunged beneath the water. More than 1,500 people had died. And the ship's crew had *known* that they were in dangerous waters!

"But...but why were we going so fast?" one person managed to ask.

Officer Lightoller looked away. He had no answer for that.

Not all the passengers on the *Carpathia* were crowded

together. One man had a full-sized cabin all to himself.

Bruce Ismay, director of the White Star Line, stayed alone in the cabin of the *Carpathia*'s doctor. He ignored the many knocks on his door and refused to see anyone or to eat or drink.

As the ship made its way through the churning ocean, he stared in silence through the porthole at the white-capped waves outside.

Ismay had hoped that the *Titanic* would beat the *Olympic*'s performance on its maiden voyage. He had wanted the *Titanic* to surprise the world.

His wish had come true.

POSTSCRIPT

Only 713 people survived the wreck of the *Titanic*. Over 1,500 people died when the ship sank. Third-class passengers were the hardest hit: 417 third-class men died, along with 119 women and children. Only 174 third-class passengers were saved. None of the large families immigrating to the United States made it to the lifeboats.

THE *TITANIC'S* PASSENGERS AND CREW

The Astors. John Jacob Astor was crushed to death when the *Titanic*'s funnel collapsed. His body, covered with soot and unrecognizable, was identified by the diamond ring on his finger and the thousands of dollars he carried in his wallet.

Astor's wife, Madeleine, survived the wreck of the *Titanic*. In August 1912, she gave birth to a son and named him after his father.

The Beckers. All four Beckers survived the wreck. Nellie Becker became more nervous and emotional after the disaster. Marion Becker died of tuberculosis in 1944. Richard Becker grew up to be a singer and social worker. Ruth became an elementary-school teacher.

Harold Bride. After the *Titanic*, Bride continued working as a wireless operator on smaller ships. Later in life, he worked as a salesman and retired to Scotland.

Daniel Buckley. Buckley escaped on one of the last lifeboats to leave the *Titanic*. A woman covered him with her shawl, so the crew members loading the boat did not see him. After telling the U.S. Senate about his experiences on the *Titanic*, Buckley disappeared.

Sir Cosmo and Lady Duff-Gordon. After they were rescued by the *Carpathia*, Sir Cosmo carried out his promise to give each of the crewmen in Lifeboat Number 1 a five pound note "to start a new kit." After he had paid the men, Lady Duff-Gordon gathered all of the crewmen for a jolly group photo.

The Duff-Gordons' behavior the night the *Titanic* sank caused a scandal in England. To many, it seemed as though the Duff-Gordons were treating the men as their own personal crew. Some people claimed that Sir Cosmo must have bribed the men not to go back to pick up more survivors.

In the end, no criminal charges were made against the Duff-Gordons. After the controversy died down, they lived a quiet life and avoided all publicity.

J. Bruce Ismay. After retiring in 1913, Ismay moved to his Irish estate, where he lived a quiet, secluded life. Until the day he died, Ismay forbade anyone from mentioning the *Titanic* in his presence.

Charles H. Lightoller. Even though he was able and experienced, Lightoller was never given charge of a ship by the White Star Line. He was made a commander in the Royal Navy during World War I. After the war, he opened a guest house and ran a successful chicken farm. He also wrote a book about the *Titanic*.

During World War II, Lightoller became a hero in England. He sailed his private yacht to France and helped evacuate British soldiers trapped at Dunkirk.

Captain E. J. Smith. Though Captain Smith did not survive the *Titanic*, his memory lives on. A bronze statue of him was erected in his hometown of Lichfield, England. Its plaque describes Smith as having had "a great heart, a brave life, and a heroic death."

Certainly, Captain Smith was very brave. In fact, his bravery may have caused the wreck. Smith ordered the engines full steam ahead, even though he knew the *Titanic* was in dangerous waters.

As one investigator, U.S. Senator William Alden Smith

(no relation), later wrote, "His indifference to danger was one of the direct and contributing causes of this unnecessary tragedy."

Jack Thayer. Thayer grew up to become a successful banker and the treasurer of the University of Pennsylvania. Throughout his life, he was haunted by what he saw early in the morning of April 15, 1912.

QUESTIONS ABOUT THE *TITANIC*

• Did someone predict the wreck of the *Titanic*?

Novelist Morgan Robertson wrote a book titled *Futility* in 1898, fourteen years before the *Titanic* sank. It told the story of a huge ocean liner filled with wealthy passengers. That ship had almost the same dimensions as the *Titanic*.

In Robertson's story, the ship struck an iceberg one cold April night and sank in the Atlantic Ocean. Most of its 3,000 passengers and crew died because the ship did not have enough lifeboats.

• What was the name of the ship in Robertson's novel?

The *Titan!*

• Could the *Titanic* have missed the iceberg?

Perhaps. The fact is, First Officer Murdoch's commands made the accident worse than it should have been.

According to one shipping manual of the day, when a ship is in danger of running into something, "to turn away and slow is the surest possible way of bringing about collision." But that is exactly what Murdoch ordered the *Titanic* to do: He reversed the engines and turned to starboard. This caused the *Titanic* to drift alongside the iceberg, dooming the great ship.

If the *Titanic* had rammed the iceberg head-on, it would probably have survived the accident. Or, if the ship had kept going full steam *ahead* as it turned, it might have steered clear of the iceberg.

The combination of slowing down and turning was deadly.

• Did a "mystery ship" see the *Titanic* sinking and ignore its calls for help?

One of the most tragic things about the wreck of the *Titanic* was the fact that its crew and passengers both saw the lights of another ship close at hand. That ship, however, disappeared without coming to their rescue.

- **What ship was it?**

Many people argue that it was the *Californian,* the steamer that had sent the *Titanic* its last ice warning shortly before the accident. Without a doubt, the *Californian* was very close to the *Titanic* when she sank. Crewmen on the *Californian* even reported seeing the *Titanic*'s distress rockets. But the ship's captain, Stanley Lord, chose not to respond.

Other people argue that the "mystery ship" could not have been the *Californian.* They point out that the *Californian* was trapped in the ice all night, while the "mystery ship" steamed away before the *Titanic* sank. The *Californian* was too far away to save the *Titanic*'s passengers and crew, they argue.

It is possible that the "mystery ship" was a steamer catching seals illegally, and that even if the men on it saw the *Titanic,* they did not respond for fear of being caught breaking the law.

Whether it was the *Californian* or an illegal sealing boat, the "mystery ship" probably could have saved all the people on the *Titanic.*

- **What made the *Titanic* sink?**

No one knows for sure exactly how the collision with

the iceberg caused the *Titanic* to go under.

At first, people thought the iceberg sliced a 300-foot-long gash in the ship's side. However, a gash that large would have sunk the *Titanic* in a matter of minutes.

Recent tests of metal taken from the *Titanic* show that the steel hull had a high sulfur content, which made it more brittle than today's steel. Perhaps the iceberg poked dozens and dozens of holes in the brittle metal along a 300-foot section of the hull.

Another possibility is that pressure from the iceberg popped rivets in the *Titanic*'s hull. This would have opened up large sections of the hull, letting water spurt in.

The damaged section of the *Titanic*'s hull is two and a half miles beneath the sea. It's likely no one will ever know for sure what caused the leaks that took the *Titanic* down.

• Why did the *Titanic* have so few lifeboats?

Actually, the *Titanic* had more lifeboats than the law called for. British law in 1912 based lifeboat requirements on a ship's size—not how many people were on board. The *Titanic* fell into the largest category of ship and legally needed only sixteen lifeboats. The laws had been written in the late 1800s, when ships as big as the *Titanic* were unthinkable.

After the *Titanic* disaster, the laws were changed. From then on, every ship had to have space on its lifeboats for every single passenger and crew member.

• Why were many of the lifeboats lowered only half full?

At first, many passengers were afraid to board the small lifeboats. They felt safer on the giant ship, even though it was sinking.

Also, crew members were afraid the lifeboats would collapse before reaching the water if there were too many people on board. Instead of lowering fully loaded boats, the crew lowered the boats half full and told them to wait nearby for more passengers. None of the boats stayed, and hundreds of lives were lost.

The *Titanic*'s crew did not know that the boats had been tested: each could safely have held sixty-five people while hanging from the davits.

• What treasures sank with the *Titanic*?

Perhaps the single most valuable object on board was a jewel-encrusted copy of the *Rubáiyát of Omar Khayyám,* an ancient book. Also, the wealthy passengers in first class traveled with money and fine jewelry, most of which was lost with the ship.

There is a chance that a vast treasure of precious metals was on the *Titanic*. After the wreck, the *Titanic*'s storekeeper recalled loading bars of gold and silver on board. These could have been balance-of-trade payments from England to the United States. The official records between the countries will not be opened until 2012.

Of course, the greatest treasures on board the *Titanic* were the passengers and crew. The loss of 1,500 lives—from presidential advisers and wealthy industrialists to eager and talented immigrants—was truly devastating to the United States and to the world.

• Will the *Titanic* ever be raised?

Already, loads of debris from the wreck have been brought to the surface—including lumps of coal, bottles of beer, light fixtures, bathtubs, and more.

In the summer of 1996, an expedition tried to raise a nine-ton piece of the hull. They lifted the piece to within a few hundred feet of the ocean's surface. Then it broke away and sank again to the ocean floor.

Many people oppose the efforts to raise the hull. They believe the *Titanic* should remain peacefully in its final resting place, two and a half miles beneath the waves.

Others feel the *Titanic* is cursed and will remain at the bottom of the ocean forever, no matter what people do to raise it.

What do you think?

ELEVATION

THE WHITE STAR STEAMER "TITANIC"

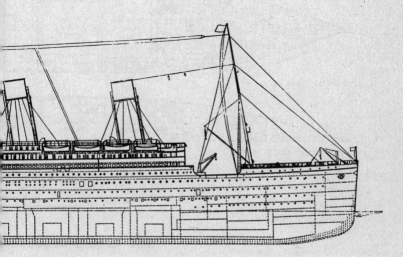

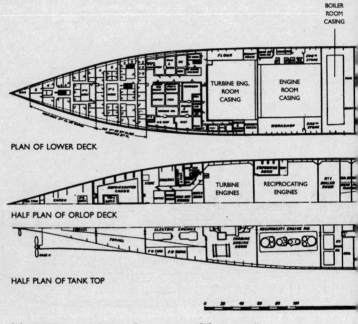

BOILER
ROOM
CASING

TURBINE ENG.
ROOM
CASING

ENGINE
ROOM
CASING

FLOUR

WORKSHOP

PLAN OF LOWER DECK

TURBINE
ENGINES

RECIPROCATING
ENGINES

REFRIGERATED
CARGO

CARGO

STORE

HALF PLAN OF ORLOP DECK

ELECTRIC ENGINES

TURBINE
ENGINE
ROOM

RECIPROCATING ENGINE RM.

TUNNEL

FUNNEL

HALF PLAN OF TANK TOP

THE WHITE STAR STEAMER "TITANIC"

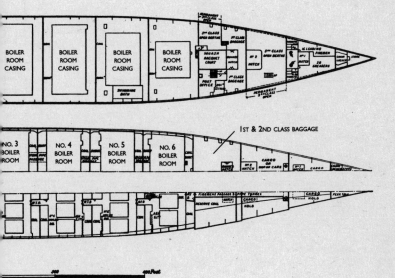

BOILER ROOM CASING

BOILER ROOM CASING

BOILER ROOM CASING

BOILER ROOM CASING

SWIMMING BATH

POST OFFICE

SQUASH RACQUET COURT

1ST CLASS BAGGAGE

2ND CLASS OPEN BERTHS

1ST CLASS BAGGAGE

NO. 1 HATCH

2ND CLASS OPEN BERTHS

NO. 1 HATCH

16 LEADING FIREMEN

30 GREASERS

PERMANENT 3RD CLASS OPEN

NO. 3 BOILER ROOM

NO. 4 BOILER ROOM

NO. 5 BOILER ROOM

NO. 6 BOILER ROOM

COAL

1ST & 2ND CLASS BAGGAGE

CARGO OR MOTOR CARS

NO. 2 HATCH

CARGO

RESERVE COAL

FIREMENS PASSAGE

CARGO HOLD

PIPE TUNNEL

CARGO HOLD

PEAK TANK

500   1000 Feet